Richard the Lionhearted

Joanne Jessop

Illustrated by Martin Salisbury

The Bookwright Press
New York · 1989

Great Lives

Beethoven
Louis Braille
Julius Caesar
Captain Cook
Marie Curie
Charles Dickens
Francis Drake
Einstein
Queen Elizabeth I
Queen Elizabeth II
Anne Frank
Gandhi
King Henry VIII
Helen Keller
Joan of Arc

John F. Kennedy
Martin Luther King, Jr.
John Lennon
Ferdinand Magellan
Karl Marx
Mary Queen of Scots
Mozart
Napoleon
Florence Nightingale
Elvis Presley
Richard the Lionhearted
William Shakespeare
Mother Teresa
Tchaikovsky
The Wright Brothers

First published in the United States in 1989 by
The Bookwright Press
387 Park Avenue South, New York NY 10016

First published in 1989 by
Wayland (Publishers) Limited
61 Western Road, Hove, East Sussex BN3 1JD, England

Library of Congress Cataloging-in-Publication Data
Jessop, Joanne
    Richard the Lionhearted by Joanne Jessop.
        p. cm. – (Great lives)
    Bibliography: p.
    Includes index.
    ISBN 0–531–18287–8
    1. Richard I, King of England. 1157–1199 – Juvenile literature.
2. Great Britain – History – Richard I, 1189–1199 – Juvenile
literature. 3. Great Britain – Kings and rulers – Biography – Juvenile
literature. 4. Crusades – Third, 1189–1192 – Juvenile literature.
    I. Title.   II. Series: Great lives (New York, N.Y.)
DA207.J47   1989   89–778
                                                         CIP
                                                          AC

Phototypeset by Kalligraphics Ltd, Horley, Surrey
Printed in Italy by G. Canale C.S.p.A., Turin

Contents

The hero king

Richard I of England is best remembered as the hero king whose glory on the battlefield won him the title *Coeur de Lion* – the Lionhearted. Richard the Lionhearted, more than any other king of England, captured the spirit of his age and stirred the imagination of future generations. Through the years this legendary figure has been linked with the brave deeds of the crusader knights, the romantic tales of chivalry and the adventures of Robin Hood. But what is the truth behind the legend?

History shows that Richard the Lionhearted was indeed a striking

Right *Richard sets out on crusade.*

Below *Richard I and his barons.*

figure – a tall, handsome knight and the most famous crusader in medieval Europe. He was also a poet, musician and scholar. But there was a darker side to Richard's character. He spent his early life feuding with his father, and in war he could be cruel as well as courageous.

As king of England, Richard showed little interest in the country or people he ruled. He used England mainly as a source of income to finance his military exploits elsewhere. His main concerns were fighting crusades in the Holy Land and defending his ancestral lands in France. These preoccupations kept him away from England throughout most of his reign. He spent only six months in England during his ten years as king. In fact, Richard the Lionhearted was an English king who could not speak English.

Nevertheless, Richard won a special place in the hearts and minds of his English subjects that has lasted to this day. It must be remembered that in the light of his own times Richard was an ideal king – the brave and noble knight who became an inspiration to his people.

Heir to Aquitaine

Richard the Lionhearted was born on September 8, 1157 at Oxford in England. He was the second son of Henry II of England and Eleanor of Aquitaine. Henry II was a great king who ruled over the vast Angevin Empire, which included most of what is today France as well as England.

When Richard was ten years old, Henry and Eleanor separated. Eleanor returned to her home in Aquitaine, a large province in southern France, taking young Richard with her. As second son, Richard was to inherit the Duchy of Aquitaine, his mother's family possession.

Eleanor's court in Aquitaine was an exciting and romantic place for a young boy growing up. It was here that the new ideals of chivalry and courtly love were being discussed and developed. Young men were encouraged to respect women and do good deeds to please them. These romantic

Richard was educated at his mother's court in Aquitaine. He became an accomplished scholar as well as a poet and musician.

themes were taken up and elaborated upon by the minstrels and troubadours who roamed the countryside.

Richard's education reflected the chivalrous ideals of the time. He learned to read and write in several languages and to compose music and poetry. As part of his knight's training he participated in tournaments, which were mock battles fought on horseback. Richard excelled as both a scholar and a warrior, and showed great promise of becoming an ideal knight.

When Richard was eleven years old, he paid homage to the king of France. This was a formal ceremony in which he accepted the king as his overlord. In return, Richard's position as heir to Aquitaine was recognized by the king of France. At this ceremony Richard was betrothed to the Princess Alice of France, but because they were both children, the marriage was not expected to take place for several years. Richard returned to Aquitaine and to his knight's training.

The rebellious son

King Henry II, Richard's father, was a great king who carried out many reforms during his reign.

Just before his fifteenth birthday, Richard was enthroned as Duke of Aquitaine. But although Henry II granted land and titles to Richard and his brothers, he gave them no authority to govern. This was a very frustrating situation for them and they plotted against their father to gain control of their inherited lands. At sixteen, Richard led a campaign against his father.

It must be remembered that in medieval times war was considered to be almost a sport. A campaign consisted of a few skirmishes. If a prisoner of rank was taken, he was treated well and then ransomed. Therefore, an enemy was worth more alive than dead. War was hardest on the poor working people. It was their houses and fields that were destroyed in battle, and they were more likely to be killed since they were not worth ransoming.

In the battles between Richard and Henry, father and son were not trying to kill one another. Richard led a battle against his father's army, not against his father in person. On one occasion when Richard's forces were chasing his father's out of a burning town, Richard galloped ahead without weapons and at great personal risk to make sure no harm was done to his father.

In the end, Richard was forced to ask for pardon from his father. Father and son made peace, and Henry then gave Richard the task of subduing the rebellious barons of Aquitaine. For the next few years Richard displayed extraordinary military skills in bringing them to heel. By the age of twenty-one he was established as a leader of first rank, famous throughout Europe.

In 1183, when Richard was twenty-five, his older brother died, making Richard heir to the English throne. Then in the summer of 1187, news reached Europe that was to change Richard's life – Jerusalem had been captured by Saladin, the great leader of the Muslim Turks, known as Saracens.

Aged sixteen, Richard led a battle against his father's army.

Taking the Cross

A soldier going on crusade wore a red cross to show he was fighting a holy war for Christianity.

Jerusalem is an important holy place for Christians. It is the city where Jesus Christ was crucified. Since the first century AD, pilgrims from all over Christendom had traveled to the Holy Land to visit Jerusalem and its holy shrines. However, by the eleventh century, bands of invading Muslim Turks, called Saracens, began to attack and kill Christian pilgrims. In response to this situation, the Pope, who was head of the Christian Church throughout Europe, called for a holy war to drive the Saracens from the Holy Land. A soldier who fought in this holy war wore a red cross on his clothes to show he was fighting for Christianity. He was called a crusader, after the Latin word *crux*, meaning cross.

During the first crusade, which set out in 1096, Jerusalem was captured from the Saracens. However, Jerusalem was also an important religious city for the Muslims and they continued to fight to regain control. In 1187 Jerusalem was conquered by the famous Saracen leader, Saladin.

When news of the fall of Jerusalem reached Richard, he immediately vowed to go on a

Above Crusaders setting sail on the journey to the Holy Land.
Below Crusaders on horseback.

crusade. This was known as "Taking the Cross," because when a man made such a vow he was handed a piece of material cut in the shape of a cross to be sewn on his clothes. For Richard this was not merely an opportunity for adventure and prestige but also a religious act.

Going on a crusade involved a great deal of preparation; armies, horses, weapons and ships needed to be organized. Richard was still preparing to go on crusade eighteen months later when another important piece of news reached him. His father, Henry II, was dead. Richard was now King Richard I of England.

Richard I of England

Above *Richard's coronation.*

Richard was crowned king of England on September 3, 1189 at Westminster Abbey, London, in an elaborate ceremony that has become the model for coronations of English sovereigns ever since. Richard was a handsome, knightly figure as he stood before the altar in his robes of office and his great crown, which was so heavy that two earls stood by his side and helped to take the weight. He swore as king to maintain the peace of the Church, to suppress injustice and to promote equality and mercy.

Richard's first act as king was to release all the people under arrest for crimes against the Forest Laws. These were the laws of the time that applied to those areas of land, called "forests," set aside as hunting grounds for the king. Anyone caught taking anything without permission was severely punished, in some cases even hanged, whether it was for seizing wood for fuel or animals for food. Richard also ruled that anyone outlawed because of offenses against the Forest Laws

In medieval England, anyone caught hunting in the king's forests was severely punished; some were hanged.

could return home safely, without fear of arrest.

This act of pardon made King Richard immediately popular with his English subjects. However, Richard's main interest was not to govern his new kingdom but to go on a crusade. In order to raise money for the crusades, Richard sold the positions of high offices of state. He also granted, in exchange for money, charters to towns, giving them the right to govern their own affairs. The effect of this scheme to raise money was to free many English towns from the control of local landowners, who by tradition had ruled local affairs.

On December 11, 1189, after just three months in England, Richard returned to France, where he completed his preparations for the crusades. Men were quick to rally under the banner of the famous Richard the Lionhearted.

A delay in Sicily

Richard and his crusaders traveled overland through France to the port of Marseilles, where they set sail for the Holy Land. At that time the voyage could be made in fifteen days, but because of several delays, it was to be ten months before Richard and his men reached their final destination.

Richard's crusade sets sail on the long voyage to the Holy Land.

Richard first sailed to the island of Sicily, off Italy, where he met up with King Philip of France, who had vowed to join Richard in his crusade against the Saracens. But there were other important matters to settle in Sicily before Richard continued his voyage. Richard's sister Joan had been married to the king of Sicily, who had recently died. The new king of

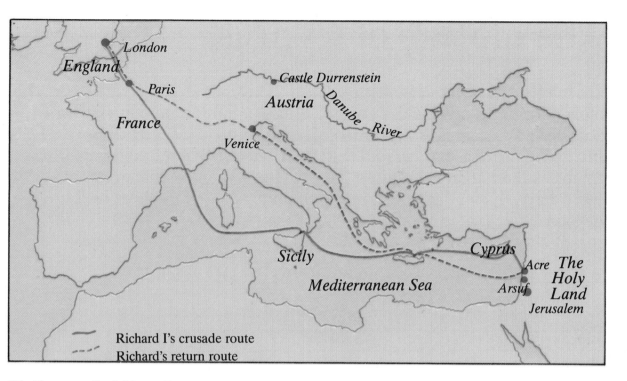

The route of Richard's crusade.

Sicily was holding Joan as a prisoner. Richard sacked the port town of Messina and forced the king to release his sister. But it was now too late in the year to sail safely to the Holy Land, and the crusaders were forced to spend the winter in Sicily.

While he was in Sicily, Richard broke his long-standing engagement to Princess Alice and became engaged to Princess Berengaria of Navarre, who had been brought to Sicily by Richard's mother, Eleanor of Aquitaine. This was a political alliance designed to ensure peace on the southern border of Aquitaine. But by breaking his engagement to the French princess, Richard had insulted the French king. This was the beginning of a rift between Richard and Philip that was to deepen over the years.

When spring arrived, the crusaders prepared to leave for the Holy Land. The French king and his army left first, followed shortly afterward by Richard. Among Richard's huge fleet was a ship carrying his sister Joan and his betrothed, Berengaria. Once again there were delays ahead.

The capture of Cyprus

On the third day out of Sicily a storm blew up, scattering Richard's fleet. Some of the ships, including the one that carried the Princess Joan and Berengaria, were driven ashore at the island of Cyprus.

The Emperor of Cyprus was an ally of Saladin and he had no intention of helping the crusaders. He offered shelter to Joan and Berengaria, but his real plan was to hold them hostage. Fortunately, before this could

A fierce storm drove part of Richard's fleet ashore at Cyprus.

happen Richard arrived on the scene to rescue his sister and his betrothed.

The island of Cyprus was vitally important as a supply line to any army invading the Holy Land. Richard realized that as long as it was held by Saladin's ally it would not be a safe base for the crusaders. Therefore, after securing the safety of Joan and Berengaria, he went on to conquer Cyprus and imprison its emperor. It took him only fifteen days to complete the conquest of Cyprus. The conquered emperor begged not to be put in irons. Richard agreed and then ordered that chains of solid silver should be made for the fallen leader.

During the campaign to capture Cyprus, Richard and Berengaria were married. Immediately after the wedding ceremony Berengaria was crowned Queen of England; however, she was destined to be the only queen who never set foot in the country.

Only when Cyprus was established as a safe haven for crusading armies did Richard once again set out for the Holy Land. This time his voyage was uninterrupted.

A 19th century illustration showing the conquered Emperor of Cyprus begging for mercy.

In July, 1191 Richard's fleet arrived at the coastal city of Acre, which was held by the Saracens but had been under siege by crusaders from Europe for several years. Outside Acre he encountered an enemy ship disguised as a French vessel bringing reinforcements and supplies to the besieged Saracens. Sinking this ship was Richard's first heroic exploit on arrival in the Holy Land.

The siege of Acre

After Richard's triumph in sinking the enemy supply ship, his arrival in Acre was greeted with a tremendous welcome by the besieging armies. The French king had arrived six weeks before Richard and had joined Duke Leopold of Austria in the two-year-old siege of Acre. But Richard brought new life and determination to the siege.

Richard was an expert on siege warfare, a skill he had learned on the battlefields of Aquitaine. He used giant catapults to shower the enemy with a deadly spray of huge stones. When he became ill with malaria, he insisted that he should be carried to the front lines on a stretcher so that he could direct the siege operations. Richard never avoided any type of military service; if needed, he would labor with his hands alongside his men. Acre soon surrendered.

Although ill, Richard continued to direct the siege operations.

But even at the time of victory, the seeds of trouble were being sown. As the crusading armies marched into Acre to take possession of the city, Duke Leopold of Austria flew his flag beside those of King Philip and King Richard as a sign of his right to share in the spoils of war. Richard did not recognize Duke Leopold's right to the loot, so he tore down Leopold's flag and trampled it into the ground. This was a grave insult, which the Duke of Austria did not forget. He sailed home in anger; his chance for revenge was to come later. Shortly after this incident, King Philip and Richard quarreled, and Philip, too, abandoned the crusades and returned home.

Richard was now in sole command of the campaign and it was his responsibility to settle the terms of the surrender of Acre. Saladin, as leader of the defeated Saracens, had agreed to pay a large sum of money and release all Christian prisoners. When Saladin failed to meet the deadline for this payment, Richard ordered the execution of the 2,700 Saracen prisoners who had been taken at Acre.

Acre surrendered, with Richard in command of the siege.

Historians have severely criticized Richard for this bloody massacre, but in the context of his time it was seen as just revenge. Even Richard's enemy, Saladin, continued to admire and respect Richard's bravery and sense of honor.

Victory at Arsuf

Two days after the massacre at Acre, Richard led his army south toward Jerusalem. Once they were in open countryside, the heavily armored crusaders had to cope with a new kind of warfare, and once again Richard proved his skill as a great military commander.

A crusading knight, covered from head to foot in chain mail with his lance, sword and shield, was a formidable opponent; no soldier could withstand the full force of a charging knight. But this style of warfare had its limitations when faced with a quick-moving Saracen horseman, armed only with his bow and arrow and razor-sharp scimitar.

On the march south Richard protected his knights from Saracen attacks by surrounding them with foot soldiers who wore arrow-proof jackets quilted with cotton. The Saracens marched beside the crusaders, a little way

The charging knights drove back and defeated Saladin's army.

inland, making sudden and unexpected attacks on the advancing army, followed by quick retreats. The foot soldiers bore the brunt of these assaults. Richard gave strict orders to his knights not to fight back but to keep in close formation.

Finally, at Arsuf, Saladin's army attacked in full force. Still Richard held his knights in line until the right moment. Then at last he gave the signal to attack; hundreds of knights charged forward, their long lances aimed at the ranks of Saracen horsemen. The enormous force of the knights' charge swept through Saladin's army, leaving thousands of his men dead in its wake.

The victory at Arsuf was one of the greatest triumphs of the crusades. Never had the crusading knights fought so well. Saladin learned that it was unwise to face a crusader knight in open battle. He had come to respect Richard the Lionhearted as the perfect enemy.

Retreat from Jerusalem

Three days after the victory at Arsuf, Richard's army marched inland toward Jerusalem. Twice Richard got within striking distance of Jerusalem, but on each occasion he gave the order to retreat, to the surprise and disappointment of his men. But Richard was a wise as well as courageous military leader. He knew that even if he succeeded in capturing Jerusalem from the Saracens, he could never hold the city.

The Saracens would never cease the fight as long as Jerusalem was in Christian hands. If the crusaders had entered and taken Jerusalem, they would have been cut off from the coast and their supplies and unable to withstand an enemy siege. The failure to capture Jerusalem was a bitter blow to Richard, but he understood the situation better than his men and accepted defeat with grace.

A peace treaty was agreed upon

between Richard and Saladin. It allowed the crusading army to keep all the territory it had captured and guaranteed the rights of all unarmed Christian pilgrims to visit Jerusalem. Many of the crusaders took advantage of this peace treaty to visit the holy city and pray before its shrines. Richard, however, refused to enter the city he was unable to conquer.

At this time, Richard received troubling news from England. His brother John, with the help of King Philip, was plotting to take over the crown in Richard's absence. It was time to go home.

Richard's crusade was over. The goal of capturing Jerusalem had not been achieved, but in spite of this he had accomplished a great deal. Richard and his crusaders had firmly established Christian control along the coastal towns of the Holy Land and gained access to the holy city itself. On October 9, 1192 Richard left for Europe, vowing to return one day to capture Jerusalem.

Richard refused to enter Jerusalem, the city he was unable to capture from the Saracens.

A king's ransom

Richard's return journey proved to be as adventurous as his outward journey. His ship was wrecked during a storm and he struggled ashore near Venice. Here Richard got word that his enemies in France, with help from King Philip, were plotting to seize him. He disbanded his army and, traveling with only a few companions, decided to risk returning to England through the territory of his enemy, Duke Leopold of Austria.

Disguised as a pilgrim returning from the Holy Land, Richard managed to reach Vienna. But the lavish spending of his page gave away his real identity. Duke Leopold saw his chance to revenge the incident of the flag. He arrested Richard and had him shut away in a strong castle, at Durrenstein, overlooking the River Danube. So great was Richard's reputation as the fearless warrior, that guards were ordered to watch him day

Returning from the Holy Land, Richard was arrested on the orders of Duke Leopold.

and night with drawn swords.

No one in England knew where Richard was being held. According to legend, it was the minstrel Blondel who discovered Richard's whereabouts. Blondel traveled from castle to castle throughout Europe singing the first verse of a song he and Richard had composed together until he heard the answering verse sung by Richard himself.

But Richard could not be rescued. A huge ransom had to be paid by the people of England before his enemies would agree to

According to legend, the minstrel Blondel discovered where Richard was being held captive when he heard the King singing the second verse of a song they had composed together.

release him. In order to raise the money, the treasures of the churches were seized and every man was forced to pay a quarter of his income. Anyone, no matter how poor, who did not contribute was imprisoned. At last the king's ransom was paid and Richard was released. In spite of these heavy demands, King Richard remained a popular hero.

25

Return to England

So feared was Richard the Lionhearted that on his return to England most of the castles held in John's name quickly surrendered without a struggle. One English knight who supported John is said to have died of fright when he heard that Richard had returned.

Only Nottingham castle offered any resistance. Its defenders held out until they were sure that Richard was really home. When they realized that it was Richard

Above *The crusaders who finally returned home were popular heroes in their own countries.*

After his release from captivity, Richard returned to England where he went through an elaborate crown-wearing ceremony at Winchester. This was designed to remove the stain of captivity and to re-assert his right to the throne. Then he had to deal with the barons who had supported John in his attempt to take the crown while Richard was away. In the meantime, John was lying low in France.

Below *On his return to England, Richard spent some time hunting in Sherwood Forest.*

26

*Richard gave his promise to
protect Robin Hood and his men.*

himself who was leading the
castle siege, they immediately
surrendered.

Richard then spent some time
in Sherwood Forest, where
according to legend, he came
upon the outlaw Robin Hood and
his followers. Robin Hood,
remembering how King Richard
had once forgiven all offenses
against the Forest Laws, asked
for a pardon. Richard gave his
promise of protection to Robin
and his men.

Richard's next task was to
regain the French territory lost
while he was away on crusade.
For this he needed money. In
order to raise funds, he dismissed
all officers of state who had
purchased their positions in 1189.
He then re-sold all the offices to
the highest bidder.

After three months in England,
Richard had raised enough
money to return to France and do
battle to recover his lost
possessions. In May, 1194,
Richard left England, never to
return again.

Death of a hero

On returning to France, Richard was approached by his brother John, who asked for forgiveness for his treachery. Richard had always been extremely fond of John and he was quick to forgive him. From then on John firmly supported Richard in his battles to regain his French territories.

Richard soon recaptured all the land lost while he was away on his crusade. During the next five years he displayed his genius as a castle-builder. He built Gaillard, the strongest castle in France,

Above *Gaillard Castle today.*

Below *John is pardoned by Richard.*

incorporating all the fortification techniques he had learned from his Saracen enemies. Gaillard became Richard's headquarters and favorite residence for the rest of his life. Its ruins on a rock overlooking the Seine River can be seen to this day.

Richard hoped that once his French domain was secure he could fulfill his vow and return to the Holy Land to capture Jerusalem. But this was not to be.

His end came unexpectedly during a minor skirmish in the French countryside. Richard had laid siege to Chalus Castle when its owner refused to hand over a treasure that Richard felt was rightfully his. While Richard was inspecting the fortification, looking for the best place to attack, he was struck by an arrow. Although it was a minor wound it soon became seriously infected.

Richard knew he was about to die and asked for the man who had shot the arrow to be brought before him. Richard forgave the man and set him free, but after his death the soldiers hanged the man who had killed their hero.

On April 6, 1199 Richard died; he was not yet 42 years old, but his name lives on in the stories and legends that tell of the brave and noble deeds of Richard the Lionhearted.

The warrior king died not in battle but from an infected wound.

Important dates

1157   Born at Oxford, England, September 8.

1167   Pays homage to the king of France; betrothed to Princess Alice.

1172   Enthroned as Duke of Aquitaine.

1173   Leads a battle against his father.

1182   Richard's older brother dies; Richard is now heir to the English throne.

1187   News of Saladin's conquest of Jerusalem reaches Europe; Richard takes the Cross.

1189   Richard is crowned king of England, September 3. Returns to France to complete preparations for the crusades, December 11.

1190–1 Sets sail from Marseilles for the Holy Land. Spends the winter in Sicily.

1191   Leaves Sicily. Captures Cyprus (April). Marries Princess Berengaria (May). Arrives at Acre (June). Acre surrenders. King of France and Duke of Austria go home (July). Massacre of Saracen prisoners at Acre (August). Defeats Saladin at Arsuf (September).

1192   Retreats from Jerusalem (September). Signs a peace treaty with Saladin (October). Leaves for Europe; arrested by Duke Leopold of Austria (December).

1194   Richard is released from captivity and returns to England, then returns to France.

1199   Wounded during skirmish at Chalus Castle and dies, April 6.

Books to read

The Age of Chivalry by Sylvia Wright (Warwick Press, 1988)

Castles by Beth Smith (Franklin Watts, 1988)

Castles and Crusaders by Philip Sauvain (Warwick Press, 1986)

Everyday Life in the Middle Ages by Fiona McDonald (Silver Burdett, 1985)

Growing Up in the Medieval Times by Penny Davies (David & Charles, 1980)

Ivanhoe by Walter Scott (Amsco Sch., 1970)

Richard the Lionheart and the Crusades by Christopher Gibb (Bookwright, 1985)

See Inside a Castle by R. J. Unstead (Warwick Press, 1986)

Glossary

Ally   A group of people or a country joined with another to fight against a common enemy.

Betrothed   Engaged to be married.

Chain Mail   Flexible armor made with interlinking metal rings.

Chivalry   The qualities of the ideal knight; they included courage, honor and a readiness to help the weak and protect women.

Courtly love   The tradition of love and formal manners towards women, as practiced by medieval knights.

Crusades   Military expeditions undertaken in the eleventh, twelfth and thirteenth centuries by the Christian powers of Europe to recapture the Holy Land from the Muslims.

Heir   A person who inherits, or is legally entitled to inherit, property or title on the death of its owner.

Holy Land   The ancient land of Palestine, now divided between Israel and Jordan.

Hostage   A person taken as prisoner by an enemy and held until certain demands are met or a ransom is paid.

Lance   A knight's thrusting weapon. It had a long wooden shaft and a sharp metal spearhead.

Medieval   Relating to the Middle Ages, about AD 1000 to AD 1500.

Minstrel   A wandering musician of medieval times who made his living by singing and reciting poetry, usually to the accompaniment of a harp or a lute.

Muslim   A follower of the Islamic religion as revealed by the prophet Muhammad.

Overlord   A nobleman or lord who ranks above another nobleman.

Pilgrim   A person who travels to a holy place or shrine as a religious act.

Ransom   To set free from captivity on payment of money; also the price paid for release of a person held captive.

Scimitar   A short, razor-sharp, curved sword used by the Saracens.

Shrine   A place of worship usually centered around a sacred object or the burial place of a holy person.

Siege   The act of surrounding a town or any fortification, with the intention of capturing it.

Tournament   A medieval sport in which knights on horseback tried to unseat one another with lances.

Troubadour   A singer in medieval times who composed and sang his own verses, which were usually about love and chivalry.

Picture acknowledgments
Ancient Art & Architecture Collection (frontispiece), 11 (above) 12, 23; BBC Hulton 8, 11 (below), 19, 24, 26 (above and below); The Bridgeman Art Library 4; The Mansell Collection 28; Mary Evans Picture Library 17, 28 (below). Map on page 15 by M. Walker.

31

Index